Beyond Borders Literary Journal
Volume 2

Editorial Team

Thomas Ray Garcia, Fiction & Nonfiction

Daniel Mendoza, Poetry

Rebecca Rodriguez, Artwork & Photography

Beyond Borders Books

Pharr, Texas

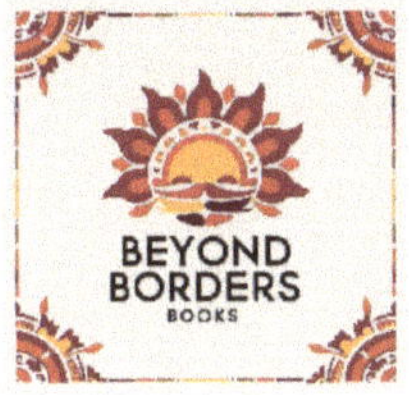

Beyond Borders Literary Journal: Volume 2

Copyright © 2025 Beyond Borders Books

ISBN: 979-8-218-86178-0

Beyond Borders Books

Pharr, Texas

beyond-borders-books.com

@beyondbordersbooks_

Cover design by Rebecca Rodriguez

First Edition, Printed in the United States of America

ACKNOWLEDGEMENTS

This 2nd issue of the *Beyond Borders Literary Journal* is only possible because of folks like you who continue to believe in the power of literature and art to change minds.

Thank you to Daniel Mendoza and Rebecca Rodriguez for serving as our poetry editor and photography & artwork editor, respectively.

Thank you to all the creative artists who submitted work to our 2nd issue of our literary journal. It takes tremendous courage to submit work, and I deeply appreciate your willingness to share your creativity with Beyond Borders Books.

Thank you to our 17 contributors for making our 2nd issue a success.

Thank you to all who purchase and read our Beyond Borders Books publications. The future looks bright for our independent press thanks to you.

Thomas Ray Garcia
Founder, Beyond Borders Books
November 2025

Table of Contents

STRAY

Martin Marizcal

He was heading south on 10th Street in the night when he saw it move. The wipers flicked the rain and he barely managed to avoid it. He threw his eyes at the rearview and saw that yes, it sat perfectly centered on the left lane, alive but staying put. He turned his eyes forward and took a deep breath.

He followed the U-turn and came back around and slowed to a stop at the second turnaround. Even where he sat it was still some distance away, this small bobbing blob at once haloed and enshrouded by the dirty streetlamp. Some distant headlights bearing down fast toward him. He looked about. Cattycorner from him, a grassy knoll with a bit of untended asphalt, a driveway that led into further darkness. Next to that, a cosmetics school. He shot forward and onto the patch of grass. From the center console he unearthed a flashlight and turned it on and it flickered off. He smacked it once, twice, a cool bluewhite beam blinded him. He set it aside. He found some scratchy white towels and he took them and the flashlight and he stepped out. He walked around to the trunk and pulled open the hatch and slouched under it. From the cargo bay he grabbed his hi-vis raincoat and pulled it on. He secured the zipper and buttons and shut the hatch and turned away.

Cars coming closer now. He ran carefully across the rainslick road. In the halo of the dull amber streetlamp the needling rain glistened like a homunculus meteor shower and under that cold pinprick barrage he saw the creature on its belly looking around at the nothing beside it. He flashed his lamp at it and stuttered his step. He saw blood. He scooped it up and ran back to the car, and close behind him the wet hiss of tires roaring suddenly to life and receding just as fast. He opened the hatch again and now sheltered under it he removed his coat and set it down flat and sat the creature down on it gently as he could. The bay's light was a duller amber and insufficient. He beamed the creature again with his lamp and saw it was a kitten. It could not be more than a few weeks old. Splotched in white and gray and orange and just a bit of black. A calico baby. He saw the blood again and now closer it looked pale white in the lamplight. He studied one of its eyes and felt sick suddenly.

He killed the torch, the blood now a faint rouged obsidian. The kitten let out a strong meow, somehow.

He dried the kitten with the towels, perhaps not gently enough, though he tried. He apologized profusely, then again in Spanish. He dried its tail, its little paws, tried to reach its tummy without squeezing too hard. He was even more deliberate with its little head, with its eye. He tucked it in the coat and closed the hatch and got back behind the wheel and drove.

He hit a red light at Wisconsin and he called his parents and let them know, that they might be ready when he arrived. The kitten meowed, the wipers squealed. The light turned green and he and his fellow nightfarers drove forward. He considered the rescue just now. He had always wondered how people online found strays and it occurred to him that he rarely heard about the rescues in poor health. Well, who really wants to hear about the tragedies? And this one, no mother, no siblings. Alone in the rain in the middle of the street. A gentle hum from somewhere as he passed Dove. It meowed again, a little softer this time. Was it that hurt or tired that it made no effort to fight him off? Its legs seemed fine, but then the light was not great nor did he assess it thoroughly. He thought again of its eye. If he kept it, if it maybe got better. If and if and if. Things could get very expensive very fast. He thought some more and he thought that that humming sound was lovely and then the rumble strip jolted him back. He lifted his glasses and rubbed one eye, then the other, apologized again to the kitten. He adjusted the heater and the wiper speed and drove on, and all the way home the kitten's strained cries accompanied the metronomic rain and the lulling tires.

Now in the kitchen he saw how much worse it was. The skin of its chin pulled down and loose like a worn-out band-aid, nor could it close its mouth. Its left eye like a discolored black pearl bulging well out of its socket. Some blood above the eye, a scrape. The other eye seemed fine, as did the legs. He tried to stand the kitten but it softly collapsed each time. And curious how the poor thing seemed unable to lift its head, how it simply sat lowshouldered and exhausted. His parents each with their own surprised and wincing faces. The kitten was cold and wet and shivering. While they disagreed on the severity of the injuries he took the baby into the restroom. The other two cats sat at the stairs, their ears perked and eyes alert, smelling an interloper. He told his parents to watch out for them as they would naturally be curious and he shut the door.

Warm water in the sink. He was gentle about the mouth, tried not to pull the flap back further. He made a ring of soap around its neck and scrubbed its body up and down, por si las pulgas. The water that ran down ran soapy and gray. Bits of dirt, or was it fleas, and did it really matter? Tried to rub the bloodied eyebrow with a light wet finger. He could smell the meat of it, raw, bloody. Flashbacks to carnes asadas, the milanesa he had made earlier that week. He tried holding his breath and it only made him sicker. In between shallow breaths he spoke to it gentle reassurances in Spanish, and he meant it all too. Whatever strength it had to meow earlier had left it now. Its cries came out weak and raspy, its jaw unclosing. He wondered then if the mouth was that damaged when he found it and he had simply failed to notice or whether he might not have worsened it himself after he set the kitten down in the car. An unsettling shiver up his back now. He dismissed the thought only not very well and on his next inhalation his stomach threatening to evacuate his percolating guilt. He held fast. It only needed to make it through the night. In the morning when the vets opened, he would take it and things would be better.

Again, in the kitchen. His dad at the threshold shooing the other cats come to study the new one up close. His mom went about wanting to boil some shredded chicken but he objected. He cupped the kitten with his hand at its chest and fed it water with a syringe, angled its head up that the water passes easier. Some of it actually went down right. The baby cried tiredly.

Pobrecito niño, his mom said.

Es niña, he said.

¿Cómo sabes? his dad said.

Los cálicos casi siempre son hembra. Un gatito cálico es bien raro.

Pobrecita niña, his mom said.

His dad brought a cordless hair dryer and they set it on low heat and worked it on the baby's body. He ran a kitchen towel on the lingering damp bits of fur and wrapped the baby in a dry towel or cloth and fed it more water, and still it cried.

¿Dónde lo encontraste? his mom asked. ¿Y la mamá?

En el medio de la calle. Literal, manejé sobre ella. Estaba sola.

Se ve muy mal, amor.

Sí. Yo sé.

¿Le pegaste tú?

No, he said. But he considered the possibility anyway. No, no fuí yo.

His dad grabbed a flapless egg box and made a bed for the baby with bubble wrap and rags. His dad said, Se ve muy mal, hijo. Igual y no la libra. ¿Qué harás?

No sé, he said. Mañana en la mañana la llevo a la Freddy Gonzalez a ver que dicen.

Bueno. Pero prepárate a tener que dormirla. Ta muy cabrón que la libre.

Sí.

¿Tienes dinero? ¿Crédito tan si quiera? his mom asked.

He casually ran numbers in his head: ignore that already late payment, avoid going out for a week, carry the one…

He said: Sí. Todavía hay.

He took the baby in its box to his room and set it down under his lamp on his nightstand and he turned the lamp on. Indirect heat but better than nothing, better than the cold rain. She hardly cried now, a hoary whisper. Or a premature death rattle, perhaps.

He changed into his sleepwear and settled into bed, watching the box, hearing the baby moving somehow, weakly pawing at the sides. He watched and though he felt too tired to sleep he nonetheless settled into a deep and restless sleep and he dreamed a memory he had long forgotten. Once, his late uncle brought his kids a little brown bunny. It came in a little cardboard box, like a Happy Meal, prize included. A cold winter then. He and his cousins played with the creature in his grandma's living room. Even in his young boy's hands the bunny felt small. Then it started convulsing. Its legs shot out straight as if frozen midstride, its body stretched out long and stiff or twisted itself or bent its back into a wide U-shape. Its little eyes frenzied and black. He held it in his arms, tried to wrap it in his sweatshirt, to warm it, to shield it from what strange force possessed it. At intervals the convulsions stopped and the bunny sat still but alert and no one knew what to do. They set the bunny back in its little box, no bigger than a child's lunchbox really, wherein it remained convulsing and resting and convulsing. Ten eternal minutes passed, then it stopped. And then he wept.

When he woke the baby was quiet. From above his blackout curtain gray dawnlight broke through, but only just. He showered and readied himself, let the warm water wash away the bitter dream. Back in his bedroom he studied her under the amber lamplight. She had actually managed to sleep. The bad eye still blueblack and burst and he thought he could see the tendrils of the optic nerve, spidery and colored a deeper darker purple. The blood from her degloved chin had dried and flaked some. He lent her some cautious scritches behind the ears. She stirred and immediately cried and looked around with her prostrate's neck. Baby alone. No mother no siblings.

Down in the kitchen he fixed himself a delicious breakfast he could not savor to sate a hunger he could not feel. A tall tumbler topped with medium roast coffee and wholesale Irish creamer. He looked out the door to overcast skies and he sipped his drink. She was still in her box up in his room but he did not hear her now. Would she even make it to the clinic today? He took another sip. The coffee was hot and it did not warm him.

It was fresh outside. He set the box down on the passenger seat and fastened the seatbelt and turned the buttwarmer on low. His mom kissed him goodbye and crossed his forehead and prayed and he drove away.

A good forty-five-minute drive to Freddy Gonzalez. He passed other early risers. He drove calmly and he kept the speed limit. He looked her over in her box and she hardly moved. He lent her his right hand that she might feel his warmth and only then did she cry a raspy meow. He spoke to her in Spanish some words of support and consolation as he himself was once spoken to in his aggrieved hours—words of love, rich and earthy and lilting. Ya, bebé, he told her, ahorita te arreglan. A ticklish tongue nuzzled his hand, a hoarse cry followed. He stifled a cry of his own. Los doctores te compondrán, he said. Ya no llores.

A fine mist as he passed by Scooter's Coffee now. He sipped his own coffee and he thought. Almost there. Running the numbers again. The cold arithmetic practiced by those who hold power over the life of another. The initial visit, the superficial observations, the tests and x-rays and medicines and overnight stays, surgery and its pursuant medicines, loss of the eye, further exams, special diet, IV fluids, another surgery likely, physical therapy not unlikely, round the clock attention once she came home, if she came home, and would the other cats take to her? All amounted to… a lot. So much more than he was equipped to handle.

Or the alternative.

At the stoplight now, waiting for the left turn arrow. His hand still around her cool body and though she still breathed she no longer cried. He sipped his coffee and he took a deep breath and he tepidly exhaled and with that release came also the truth. What his coward's heart knew even before he went to sleep the night before. Before he sat an hour in the lobby with her in her box, before waiting in the small room with the cold aluminum table where the nice doctor would point out the apparent muscular damage of her sunken neck, the burst eye and peeled chin being in fact of lesser concern, before she the doctor would frankly but not unkindly tell him that the baby's odds were fifty-fifty at best and that should he want to try and save her things would get very expensive very quickly, and before the doctor and nurse waited patiently on him to weakly ask them to proceed, and before he held the calico baby as she at last went limp, he knew the truth— that the best he could

offer, the most he was willing to offer her was cold mercy, but a mercy

nonetheless.

Daylen Adams, *My Next Mission*

How to Skin a Civilization

Alexis M Levine

I was gold before they made me dig it—
the smelter, not the mine.
Architect of pyramids, they renamed *"unknown."*
Now they weigh my worth in carats, not kingdoms.

I was a library, my shelves heavy with truth,
before they burned my scrolls,
called me illiterate,
then fed my stories to their children
as *"discovery."*

They dressed me in their lace,
stitched over scar-tissue skin,
traded my mother's name for a passport.
Their mirrors sneer: *"Almost human."*

They dig my children's graves
and call it *"progress."*
A trophy in their museum of conquest.

A MEASUREMENT FOR DISTANCE

Richard Quiroz

Sometimes we measure distance by time,

Instead of miles, or kilometers, or the number of stops for rest,

Or the number of towns you pass, or their remnants,

Or the number of broken windows counted,

From an abandoned schoolhouse, From a broken-down rusty car,

From a hollowed-out gas station, From a rotting house with no door

where,

A young face once looked out to daydream,

Of the road stretched before them, leading to a bridge,

Where a busted guardrail now hangs,

Next to a white cross, a reminder

That places   can always   haunt you.

Think of why that is, every time you pick up and go settle,

Someone else's home,

Taken from those made from the very same earth,

Concrete is poured into,

For billboard signs wider than the size of the sides of

houses,

Surrounded by wildflowers, yet from seeds spewed by

tractors on the edges,

Of mowed strips of grass leading up to barbed wire fences,

The border for plots, acres, lots, all parceled land

Developed meticulously, and accordingly from plans,

Drawn yesterday but adapted,

From blueprints centuries ago

For expansion and growth

To keep moving and building

Like a fire ant colony as deep as the core of the earth.

We now live in someone else's afterthought:

"They'll have to leave eventually."

Never did they understand what it's like

To be seen as overgrown weeds in the path for a flowerbed,

To be uprooted,

To learn how others see your removal as a sign of

"progress,"

A word with many definitions,

From someone else's own invention.

        Once you've understand the permanence of the words,

"Tanto la tierra   como la gente   estan vivas,"

You will know those who built their lifetimes for one another.

Generation by Generation and strong as bricks

Made from the very same clay

From the land their mothers and fathers worked.

This has always been,   and will be   Inherent

In the hearts of the shadows in my memories.

Robinson Lopez, *Las Animas*

WHY I WAIT BY THE RIVER

Luis Lizardo-Rodriguez

Mi vida,

If you're reading this—if this letter ever finds you across the veil I made between us—know that I have thought of nothing else since. My body lurches, but my mind races with thoughts of you. Though they tell our story all wrong, I don't write to be forgiven or to correct their narrative. I write in hopes of shaping yours. That you may see me not as the monster they have constructed, but the mother they wronged. Your mother.

What you have to know is this, we didn't have much. Our houses were made of what the earth allowed—sunbaked clay, patched tin, and hope. Every wall held a crack where something had once tried to grow: ivy, mold, a child's name scratched in with a stick. Out here, silence was a full-time job, broken only by the shuffle of sandals when it was harvest time.

Like clockwork, October came. Rain gave way to the sun and the heat let us know break time was over.

The soil belonged to Don Gerardo's family long before the people did. The sun rose for him, they said, and the rain waited on his crops. Whether nature worked for him or not, we sure did. The men wiped sweat with the same shirts they worked in. The women tied their braids tighter and passed tortillas down the line. That was life—pick, peel, pray. Pray the corn was fat. Pray the river didn't rise too soon. Pray.

Some may hear this and feel pity, but we took refuge in the little things. The steam rising from a fresh tortilla. The way a baby stopped crying when their grandmother sang the right lullaby. A breeze that made the curtains dance like they weren't made from rags. We didn't have much, but we had rhythm. We had stories passed down like recipes, jokes that softened the silence.

"Mamá, why does Tío Jacinto always wear his hat, even when he sleeps?" asked mi hermanito, José.

"So my dreams don't fly away, mijo," he'd reply with a sly grin.

"Then why do you still wake up grumpy?" José asked.

"Because his dreams are smart enough to run," Mami said, taking down clothes from the line.

It was moments like that which made the village almost feel like a secret worth keeping. But here, even laughter had chores to do.

"No dejes para mañana lo que puedes hacer hoy." Mami would always say.

And there was always something that could be done today.

Papi worked in the city, he would send back money, but it never seemed to be enough. Mami would say how even that seemed to be drying up, each subsequent check getting thinner and thinner. The hope was that I might be sent to school, but life kept collecting its debts: Josélito's fever, the roof leaking, our mule got attacked by a coyote and ended up with a broken leg. Each time we saved a little, the world found a way to take it back.

I kept studying anyway, copying down lessons from borrowed notebooks, whispering conjugations while I shelled beans. Mami said I had a good head on my shoulders, the others in the village seemed to agree -- though not for the same reasons.

I think I first realized I was different when I was nine. *Maybe ten.* I was carrying tamales to the neighbor's house when Chucho — who always smelled like sweat and cane liquor— said something to the women who were with me. He put his hand on my head and said, "Careful with that one. Gonna break hearts." They laughed like it was harmless, but I remember the way my skin prickled, how I gripped the basket tighter and didn't know where to look. After that, eyes followed me like gnats in the heat. I didn't have the language for it then, but I started walking faster. Smiling less.

See, mi vida, everyone wants to be beautiful. The thing they will never realize is that beauty doesn't ask for permission to be seen. And when the wrong eyes notice you, it doesn't matter how many words you can conjugate. Maybe if I'd stayed small, stayed quiet, kept shelling beans—maybe I'd still be your mother in their eyes, in your eyes too.

One day, while I was hanging the wash and cursing the wind for playing games with the bedsheets, I felt someone staring. Not in that passing, curious way people sometimes look—this was heavier, like a hand pressed between my shoulder blades. I turned around, slow, expecting to catch someone turning away, pretending they hadn't been watching. But he didn't turn away. He just kept looking. His name was Cristóbal Gerardo. Now I knew of him, but had never really seen him much. He'd been sent off when we were younger. People said boarding school, then after a while people said university. Regardless of what people said, there he was—at the edge of the road with his arms crossed, looking at me like he had all the time in the world. He wasn't smiling, not exactly, but there was something amused in his face, like he knew something I didn't. The sun sat behind him, turning his white shirt near transparent, the sleeves rolled neatly to his elbows. His boots had the kind of shine no real work ever leaves behind. All of it gave him a sort of ethereal glow—like he didn't quite belong to this place. And for a moment, *I* didn't belong to myself either. When I finally came to, I managed to peel myself away. The interaction could not have lasted long, but for the rest of that day he stayed stamped to my mind.

I wasn't smitten at first, not exactly. But it was hard not to be captivated by him. He was like a silk ribbon caught on barbed wire— too out of place to ignore. I had to know what brought him here, what kept him from blowing away.

The first time we actually spoke, I was rinsing clothes by the river, the hem of my skirt damp and clinging to my ankles. I hadn't noticed him approaching—not until I looked up and saw him crouched a few paces away, not too close, just near enough to feel his presence.

"Do you always sing when you work?" he asked.

I hadn't realized I was humming. I looked at him carefully, trying to read whether he was mocking me or not. But his face didn't hold that kind of smile.

"Only when I forget someone might be listening," I said.

He chuckled—soft, genuine. "I hope I didn't ruin it."

I shook my head and kept scrubbing, slower now. "Depends who's listening."

He didn't answer right away. Just watched the water swirl past my wrists, the soap bubbles breaking.

"What were you singing?" he finally asked.

I paused. "Something mi abuelita used to sing. I don't remember the words, just the sound of it."

"That's nice," he said. "Sounds like you remember it where it matters."

I didn't know what to say to that. So I said nothing. And after a few moments, he stood and dusted his hands like he'd done something. Then he nodded and left, the same way he came—without warning.

He started coming by more often after that. At first, it was just in passing. He'd appear near the path to town, or linger by the jacaranda tree with some excuse about checking on the harvest. But his gaze always found me. And slowly I let mine find him back, with more control My throat tightened. He spoke like salvation. I wanted to believe him.

"It wouldn't be proper," I murmured.

"We'll make it proper," he said, taking my hand. "You'll want for nothing. I promise."

There was a long silence. The crickets kept chirping. My heart beat loud enough to drown them out.

"Say yes," he said, quieter now, as if afraid I'd vanish. And I did.

I moved in by the end of the month.

At first, it was almost like the stories said it would be. The bed was soft. Meals were hot. My hands were no longer cracked and Cristóbal always brought home little gifts—fabric in my favorite color, a book of poetry, dried hibiscus for tea. He kissed my forehead when I was tired. He touched my stomach like it was something sacred.

When I told him I was pregnant, he smiled. A real smile, I think. He kissed me hard and lifted me into the air like in those old movies. For a while, I believed we had carved out something new—something mine. But somewhere in the swell of my belly, something else began to swell in him too. Not anger, not yet—just absence. He started staying out later. Forgot to write the letters with the money for my family. When I reminded him, he'd sigh, wave a hand, say, "Next week, mi amor. Things are tight right now."

He stopped asking how I slept. Stopped holding my hand in public. The tenderness he once carried like a badge now flickered only when others were watching. And when we were alone, the silence thickened.

"You're tired again?" he'd say. "You have one job now—how hard can it be?" Or,

"You used to hum when you cleaned. Now the house feels dead."

I told myself it was stress. That he was scared, too. That he didn't mean it.

But the things he didn't say grew louder than the ones he did. And the house—once so full of warmth—began to echo. I could feel my voice bouncing off the walls with no place to land.

My throat tightened. He spoke like salvation. I wanted to believe him.

"It wouldn't be proper," I murmured.

"We'll make it proper," he said, taking my hand. "You'll want for nothing. I promise."

There was a long silence. The crickets kept chirping. My heart beat loud enough to drown them out.

"Say yes," he said, quieter now, as if afraid I'd vanish. And I did.

I moved in by the end of the month.

At first, it was almost like the stories said it would be. The bed was soft. Meals were hot. My hands were no longer cracked and Cristóbal always brought home little gifts—fabric in my favorite color, a book of poetry, dried hibiscus for tea. He kissed my forehead when I was tired. He touched my stomach like it was something sacred.

When I told him I was pregnant, he smiled. A real smile, I think. He kissed me hard and lifted me into the air like in those old movies. For a while, I believed we had carved out something new—something mine.

But somewhere in the swell of my belly, something else began to swell in him too. Not anger, not yet—just absence. He started staying out later. Forgot to write the letters with the money for my family. When I reminded him, he'd sigh, wave a hand, say, "Next week, mi amor. Things are tight right now."

He stopped asking how I slept. Stopped holding my hand in public.
The tenderness he once carried like a badge now flickered only when
others were watching. And when we were alone, the silence thickened.

"You're tired again?" he'd say. "You have one job now—how

hard can it be?" Or,

"You used to hum when you cleaned. Now the house feels

dead."

I told myself it was just stress. That he was scared, too. That he didn't
mean it.

But the things he didn't say grew louder than the ones he did.
And the house, once so full of warmth, began to echo. I could feel my
voice bouncing off the walls with no place to land. By the time our
child was born, I had stopped asking for tenderness. I just prayed he
wouldn't turn cold.

We arrived home earlier than planned. You had fallen asleep against
my chest, your breath warm and even. I pushed the gate open slowly,

quietly, almost ashamed for sneaking into my own house. The door wasn't locked. Inside, laughter.

A woman's voice, higher, unfamiliar. And Cristóbal's, soft, coaxing, the tone he used with me when we were first falling into whatever this had become. I crept forward, heart hammering, afraid of being right. The sitting room came into view.

There she was, lounging in the robe I had stitched myself. One of his arms was thrown lazily around her waist. He fed her a grape like it was some joke, and she giggled before licking the juice from his fingers. In my arms, you stirred and so I clutched you tighter.. My breath came out in a sound between a gasp and a growl. He looked up.

The girl scrambled to cover herself, shame blooming across her face. Cristóbal, by contrast, barely flinched.

"You were supposed to be gone until Sunday," he said flatly.

"How dare you," I whispered. "How dare you bring someone into our home? Into our bed?"

The girl tried to speak, but I cut her off with a glare sharp enough to slice fruit.

"Get out," I hissed. "Now."

She grabbed her things. Cristóbal didn't move.

"What did you think this was?" he asked. "A fairytale?"

"No," I said, voice trembling. "I thought it was love. I thought it was a promise."

He stood slowly, anger rising in him like a tide. "You should be careful how you talk to me."

"I gave up everything for you."

"And now you have a child. A roof. That's more than most girls like you ever get."

The words struck harder than a fist. But what came next—

He stepped forward, and I don't know if he meant to shove me, or grab me, or just intimidate. All I know is his hand struck my face, sudden and sharp, and you (in my arms) wailed from the shock of it.

I didn't wait.

I turned and ran—out the door, down the path, not stopping even as you cried and the wind tore at my shawl.

I didn't go to the river right away.

I went home.

To my home. To the place where I learned how to thread a needle, how to tell ripe fruit by smell, how to hold in tears even when they burn behind your eyes. I hoped for warmth, a plan, a place to think. I hoped my mother would see the bruise blooming on my face and know—know—what needed to be done.

She did see it. Her eyes flicked to it like lightning, then away again.

"He hit me," I said, voice raw. "In front of her."

She didn't speak at first. Just stirred the beans on the stove like she hadn't heard me. Like steam was more important than the storm I carried in my chest.

"Mamá," I pleaded. "Say something."

Her hands moved slower now. "You should've stayed the weekend. Men don't like surprises."

"What does that mean?" I demanded.

"It means you're not the first woman this has happened to," she said quietly. "And you won't be the last."

I stepped back like her words had slapped me harder than he ever could. "So I'm just supposed to live with it? For the child?"

"For your life," she snapped. "What do you think will happen if you leave him? You'll be alone. Poor. And he'll make sure that child hates you for it."

My mouth opened, then closed. No strength to carry both my pain and hers.

"You think I don't know?" she whispered, eyes suddenly wet. "You think I don't remember what it's like to be young and full of fire? But fire won't keep you warm when the world is cold. Be smart. Go home. Say you overreacted. He'll forgive you."

Forgive me.

I held you tighter. I didn't say another word. Not when my mother kissed my child's forehead and said "He needs his father." I walked out the door, the sky was already darkening. Under the night sky, I heard the shouts first. Heard familiar voices twisted by fear and accusation. Then I saw the flicker of torches in the distance. Someone must have told them I ran. That I'd taken you. That I'd lost my mind. No one would have any reason to believe me over Gerado's golden boy, so I ran.

I reached the river, but the torches loomed through the trees on both sides of me. The only way out was through the water. I thought we might be able to carry our way through it, and escape unnoticed under the moonlight. I tried to ease us into the water, but I underestimated the river's wrath, the strength of the current. It swept my leg and we splashed into the water. With only one hand free, I struggled to stay afloat. My body begged me to let go of you, my survival instincts screaming. But I knew the second I let you go, I would never hold you again. And so, the river beat against me like it had a vendetta. My knees scraped against the jagged rocks beneath the surface. Branches clawed at my arms, tore at my clothes, left ribbons of blood behind. Water filled my mouth, ears, nose. I couldn't tell sky from current. Every stroke forward felt like ten back. I thought you slipped once and I screamed so hard I swallowed water. I clutched you tighter, felt your warmth against my chest, your weight pulling me down. Soon enough, the water overtook us both.

When I awoke, I immediately felt heaves of mud and river water being exorcised from my body. I bent over, clawing my fingers into the wet soil, and started hacking out the earthy sludge onto the bank. My body ached all over: skin torn, knees split open, ribs bruises from the river rocks. My ears rang and eyes stung, but even through the haze I immediately thought of you. I looked around wildly, heart hammering. The riverbank stretched quiet and unfamiliar in both directions. The trees swayed above me, indifferent. The river moved on like nothing had happened

"Mi vida," I said louder, dragging myself to my feet, legs trembling beneath me. "Where are you?"

No answer. Just the rush of the water and the wind in the reeds. I stumbled down the shore, scanning the rocks, water, brush. My skirt clung to me, heavy with riverweight. My arms ached with emptiness. I had to find you, you had to be here, I had to believe the river hadn't taken everything.

Then I saw *her*.

She was twisted near the rocks, soaked through, hair fanned out like black riverweed. Her dress clung to her skin, arms curled tight around nothing. She looked exactly like me, but her chest didn't rise. I tried to move toward her, to call out, but no sound came. Just a high, thin noise in my ears. I staggered back, slipping in the mud. I felt light—wrongly light, as though the weight of my body had stayed with her. That's when I heard a cry that echoed downstream. Not yours. Not quite. But close enough to twist the knife.

I turned.

A boy, maybe five, stood at the edge, stunned by what he saw. His mother called for him from up the path, her voice growing sharper with worry. But the boy was still, tears in his eyes. Eyes fixed on me. I started wading over the water towards him. When I had finally reached the other side of the bank,

I took him.

And at that moment, I understood. This was what I was now. No longer a woman, wife, or daughter.

But a mercy.

They call me a monster. Say I drown children out of spite. That I roam the banks to steal what I had lost. But I don't simply take them,

I hold them.

I shield them from the world that made me choose the river. I shield them from the current. I rock them like I did you, singing soft melodies. While you and I were beaten and battered, I make sure they

don't lose their peace in the end. I give them the only escape I ever
found.

I give them to you, because they go where I can't. Past the reeds, past
the weight of this world, past the silence that held me under. Each one
a lullaby sent ahead in my stead.

So if you ever hear my song or feel the chill of river mist on your
cheek, know it's only me. Still searching, loving you the only way I
know how. The only way I can.

Tu madre,

siempre.

I AM A "NO SABO" KID

Kendra Lara

My Spanish isn't perfect.

The way my tongue fights the flow

as I speak what was supposed to be my native language,

words never fully sounding right in my American mouth

Envious of others who can roll their r's with ease

While I sound like an engine that won't start.

rrddddrrrrddd

How my immediate response when asked if I can speak Spanish is

"No es perfecto, pero si entiendo"

Apologizing for what should have been *papitas*

An outsider in my own community, as they laugh at jokes I don't

understand

decades worth of knowledge I have little access to

I try

and try and will keep trying

but

I

am

a no sabo kid.

SoSaira

Neha Gupta

Saira's fingers flew across her mobile screen as she typed an update for her five thousand-people-strong Instagram family.

"Grinding through this 🔥 But also planning some weekend fun, 'cuz you KNOW what's on Sunday?"

5:05 PM, SoSaira

"IT'S MY 16TH BIRTHDAY!!! 🎉 🎂 And this year, I'm doing something WILD. Instead of planning ANYTHING, I'm letting YOU GUYS surprise me. Like, literally. Want to know how?! 👇"

7:22 PM, SoSaira

"Here's the deal: Everyone has to dress as... ME. But not just *any* version of me. The version *you* like, hate, love, envy... whatever! 😈 "
Adds poll: "Are you ready for the #MeParty?"
Options: "YASSS" and "OMG YES"

9:45 PM, SoSaira

"I'm talking deep cuts. Inside jokes. My weird quirks. My obsessions. The things only *you* would know. Think of it as the ultimate 'How well do you know SoSaira challenge'. 🗣️ "

10:00 PM, SoSaira

"And just so you know, I'm only re-posting the **BEST ONES**. Make 'em good. Make 'em iconic. Let the games begin. 😉 #ProveYouKnowMe #BirthdayChallenge #NoBasicBirthdays #MeParty"

10:05 PM, SoSaira

Saira kept her phone aside and felt content. The background noise of multiple pings on her Apple device meant she had the attention of many of her 5K followers. Well, soon-to-be 5K, anyway. The #MeParty would get her that. In fact, she planned on hitting 5K and announcing it during her party. She had ordered the golden balloons with a 5 and a capital K. She was now visualizing holding them in her hand and laughing in her birthday dress—an aquatic blue rushed bodycon dress paired with her favourite big gold hoops, the tiniest shoulder bag and white chunky platform heels (her mom still won't allow her to wear those "dangerously trippy" high heels, she thought moodily).

She was turning 16. She had to look the part.

When Saira was about 10 years old, her mom, Mrs. Goel began sending her to a dance studio. It conveniently came attached with a Yoga studio where *she* wanted to practise. She couldn't leave Saira home alone, and so she got her along, deposited her to the dance teacher and truly relaxed and breathed well with her Yoga buds.

Mrs. Goel wanted to do everything, at the same time. Often that led to her doing nothing, at any time. She tried to multitask and achieve all her dreams so bad that she ended up with no energy and zero patience to actually finish anything. In those frustrating, in-between moments, she would climb on her bed and reward herself for her effort and failure in the most convenient way–scrolling on the phone. Minutes would fly into hours and she'd momentarily forget the angst of tasks not done.

The trouble was, scrolling through others' carefully curated life took her away from her own life only for a bit. In the end, she felt worse. When she saw that guy cooking his mum's recipes, she romanticized cooking healthy meals for her family. But in the next minute, a sale haul post made her feel her wardrobe needed an upgrade, while a friends' weight loss journey reminded her to take better care of her body and a fourth friend's child's achievements made her realise she needed to do something for her kids.

Now this last thing–the one that involved making your child do something instead of doing something on your own–Mrs. Goel was determined to clear off her list, first.

She made a call to her mom friend and took deets on her daughter's dance classes. It appeared to be Mrs. Goel's lucky day because this call was going to get her to accomplish two things at once – work on her fitness and work on her child's growth. Oh, how she loved the instant gratification of getting two things done at once. She was the perfect example of a millennial mom–she felt truly happy and productive only when she was juggling many things at once.

Mrs. Goel, however, was soon to discover that her daughter was quite talented and expressive. The dramatic tantrums had some good use, after all, she thought as she hurried to make a new Instagram account to safekeep her daughter's dance journey.

Validation soon started pouring in and by the time Saira turned 14, Mrs. Goel decided it was time she had a phone to herself. Anyway, her daughter kept taking her own phone away too often and for too long, sometimes to shoot her dance videos and at other times, to check her homework. To top it all were her dreary online classes which often meant Mrs. Goel had to part with her phone for unbearably long stretches altogether.

And so, over the years, from mother to daughter, SoSaira grew. From 500 followers under the leadership of her mom to 5000 of her own–SoSaira blossomed into a tiny community of its own.

Saira's brain now worked in a witty way. It viewed everything from the lens of an IG story. Every event in her life was seen from how well it would be received by her followers - people she liked to believe were invested in her life. She loved the attention and it validated her teenage years.

The #MeParty was hardly an original idea, but it was new enough and perfect for her 16th birthday party.

What could possibly go wrong?

Saira changed into her cutesy pink, striped night suit set. She carefully tied her hair into a fishtail pony and added a bit of colorless gloss. At 12 AM, she expected her best friends to facetime her. Since they would screenshot it and put up a story on their 'gram, she had to look like a nonchalant princess.

"340 likes and 25 comments"
11:15 PM, SoSaira
She checked her stories again, this time reading them the way she imagined her followers would read them. All her stories sounded progressively cool to her. She happily scrolled through the new comments on her story:

@PrettyKa: *"OMG I have so many ideas for this, which one should I pick?? 😭"*

@GGame: *"You are SO iconic for this challenge! Happy birthday queen! Will reply to the sticker after I think* 🥺*"*

@Ananyaya: *"This is going to be hilarious. I'm already brainstorming my entry haha."*

@NatDoingThings: *"Good luck picking the best ones, knowing your friends lol"* Saira perked up. At last, Nat's comment. He had been watching her stories, but hadn't responded and Saira was itching to know his reaction.

"Won't you be a part of my #MeParty?" she hurriedly sent a DM to Nat. Of course, she wouldn't write this publicly. Her friends knew how hard she was crushing on him and wouldn't stop teasing her.

Three tiny dots. A reply being typed out.

"What's he writing that's taking so long? What's he re-writing THAT'S taking so long?", Saira wondered impatiently.

Finally, a reply. *"Would you want me to?"* 11:30 PM, @NatDoingThings

Wasn't it obvious? Saira thought. She wondered if she should act cool and say something casual like, "Only if you want to." But then, she remembered Pritika telling her that women should be explicit in conveying their expectations to men, if they want to have them fulfilled.

"We're not like the mute millennials, Saira." Pritika had explained to her, one day during lunch break. *"We're Gen Z. We say what we want. Women expecting men to get them flowers and the like – that's So last century. See how Amay is always giving me the perfect gifts? That's 'coz I let him know in advance."*

Taking advice from Pritika was totally sane, 'coz even though they shared the same number of years on Earth, only Pritika had been in a relationship for the past two years. She must be doing something right.

So, Saira typed, *"Of course, I can't wait to see how well you know me"* 😛

"You're on!" Nat replied and Saira's faith in Pritika's deep relationship knowledge soared.

Pritika and Ananya were facetiming her, already? Oh, it was 11:50 PM, of course they would all need 10 minutes prep time for the perfect screenshot. They were best friends for a reason; their loyalties were aligned just as well as their Instagram aesthetics were.

Lots of giggles, fake candle blow outs, hearts on the screen and promises of friendship later–Saira fell into sleep easily, fatigued from the glare of the screen and a job well done. Her followers were going to make tomorrow the most memorable day of her life.

Saira had promised herself that she'd check her phone next day only after breakfast with her parents. Mum would have pancakes and presents ready - this had been her birthday tradition ever since she was a little girl. Pancakes were the only thing that could get replaced from this setup – to whatever Saira loved that year, but everything else – mom, dad and their ready hugs and million kisses and special presents never missed a year. Not even the year her grandparents passed. It was a quiet birthday but the love was intact.

But, this year, the influencer in Saira hijacked her sleep and she found herself wide awake at 3 AM. She immediately checked her phone and saw there were just a few more likes and meaningless comments from the last time she was online. Disappointed, she kept her phone away from her bed, to avoid thinking about it. It was, as if, a greater physical distance between them was the only way to create a mental distance too. She went back to sleep. But, at 9 AM, as soon as she woke up, she scrambled up to it, and saw birthday wishes pouring in. There were still no videos of her friends and followers posing as her. She had been quietly hoping to be bombarded with these videos on waking up, but guess it was too early for people?

She heard mom calling her out from the kitchen and decided to get back to the wishes later. By the time breakfast got over, she hoped she'd finally be greeted with a #MeParty video.

Just as she hurried down the stairs, Dad told her to close her eyes. This had been their own little tradition. It started when Saira was a baby and excitedly tore away at her gifts. But, all these years later, she liked playing along. So, she closed her eyes and on her Dad's cue, opened them to see a cute Stanley cup, standing in all its glory on their kitchen top.

Saira could already imagine beginning her dance videos by gracefully sipping from her Stanley in one. It was the perfect gift! She flew into Dad's arms.

"There's one more thing, for our dancing star!" Mom said and Saira noticed a beautifully packaged box with a bow, waiting patiently for its turn, to catch her attention.

"Please record this for me, Dad" Saira chirped happily as she unwrapped the gift box. She knew it was good for engagement to look casual and unprepared, sometimes. It made her feed more relatable. Anyway, this video would only go up as story for 24 hours and not grace her feed as a post, she calculated as she slowly unwrapped the box.

She acted extra excited in front of the camera and then revealed a cutsey phone cover that could be hung around now as a sling.

"Oh mom, it's just what I wanted", she said as she flaunted her Stanley Cup and phone cover sling. She ran upstairs to put on her sling cover on her phone. She noticed a new video mention by @GGame thought to herself that the day just kept getting better.

"Bua, Fufu, Dadi, Dadu, Nanu and Nani are coming home for dinner tonight, for

your birthday, Saira…" Mom's voice trailed behind.

"Yes, yes", Saira replied, distracted with her shiny new gifts and impatient to put them to use at once.

She thanked her parents and carried her gifts in her arms upstairs, into the privacy of her own room. She picked her favourite corner of the bed–the one with the charging station and eagerly open @GGame's video.

He had recorded a video of himself, dressed in a pink top, riding his bicycle at full speed. Right outside their tuition classes, he suddenly brakes, almost falling off his cycle. A Bollywood song blasts in the background as he now enters the class full of students with a dramatic hair flip.

Saira laughed hard before realizing she was laughing at her own self. But it was so funny and typical of GG.

"You got that right — I'm totally dramatic! 💅 *But don't you love me more for it?"*
@GGame

11:30 AM, @SoSaira
Soon, her Apple device got busy reminding her of the many people who were mentioning her in their stories.

It seemed like the best birthday ever, as Saira spent hours devouring the attention of her friends and followers, replying and re-posting and thanking people for their wishes and the #MeParty videos. She felt like a celebrity and she loved every bit of it.

A follower she hadn't met in person, but had had many conversations in DM posted a video copying her dance style. Her bestie Ananya posted a video of a makeup tutorial – complete with Saira's accent and hairstyle.

Pritika had made a reel of some of their most adorable moments and signed it off by saying "Let's get into it, fam" – just the way Saira addressed her followers. Saira endless reposts were a testimony to her popularity as a beloved content creator.

Suddenly, something caught her attention, as scrolled through people's stories. Inayat from Section A2 had posted something that was being shared by others. She hadn't expected Inayat to post her a birthday message. Nothing had happened between them and they never really talked but Saira always felt like Inayat didn't like her. Maybe it was the way Inayat always followed every story she posted, but never once liked them. In fact, despite keeping this steady gaze on her, Inayat acted as if she didn't know Saira when they crossed paths in school.

'Bold of people to assume anyone would actually want to 'post like them.' #MeParty.

"

Saira was shocked. Was this aimed at her? She scrolled down to see this post had actually received many likes and some of Inayat's friends had gone on to share and put their two bits on it.

"So Cringe!"

"YAWNNN!!"

"Pretty sure she copied this idea, like she copies all her dance moves. What's the opposite of GOAT? Does it begin with an S?"

Saira felt breathless. She felt so heavy in the chest that for a moment, she had to keep her phone down to let herself believe that none of this was being said to her face.

She grabbed her phone again and tried to make sense of these posts. She felt so angry that she decided to reply to each one of these comments. But just then, she saw Nat had liked this thread!

Saira blinked and felt her heart sink to the bottom of her stomach.

She re-checked. It was Nat, all right. In fact, only now did she notice a story mention from Nat. She opened the video and saw Nat in his school uniform, outside the school gate. Suddenly, Inayat arrives and starts heaving and drooling all over him and repeats *'Oh, Nat, I love you. Look at me. Talk to me. Kiss meee!!* In the background, Nat's friends shout, *"Twerk for him, Saira and he's yours!!"* The video ends with all of them howling uncontrollably with laughter.

Saira had never felt so ashamed in her life. Was this what people thought of her? Why had Nat gone along with this demeaning video KNOWING the feelings she had for him?

She didn't know what was worse—the humiliation, the rejection or the disgrace she felt. She switched off her phone, locked her door, closed the lights and cried hard into her pillow. She never wanted to step out of her room, again.

A few terrible minutes passed where she contemplated changing her school, confronting Nat, giving Inayat a befitting reply through an equally humiliating video. Reflexively however, she reached back to her phone, switched it on, digested all the hate being spewed at her and called Pritika and Ananya. She hadn't meant to cry as soon as they picked up her call, but the tears flowed out of her at a volume she was surprised at. She hadn't realized how deeply she was feeling affected till her friends also expressed their horror at what was unravelling on Instagram.

"... and, to do all this, on her birthday. That's just so mean..." Ananya voiced

her confused thoughts, which made Saira sob even harder.

"Just report their content as hate," Pritika suggested.

".. and suffer their mockery? Tomorrow is Monday, how will I face anyone at school?" Saira wailed and then asked her besties *"… Maybe I should delete my own posts. Let the whole thing go down and be forgotten."*

"No one is going to forget this," Ananya blurted out and instantly regretted it. She didn't want to make Saira's birthday worse than it was already turning out to be, but the problem seemed too enormous for her tiny limited experience in dealing with adult matters like bullying.

The thought that no one was going to forget it haunted Saira. She abruptly disconnected the call, switched off her phone and hid inside a blanket. She started shivering and sobbing. She didn't know how to control the strange sensations that gripped her body. She felt she was under another's control and rocked herself back and forth aimlessly, till she fell into a dreamless sleep.

Loud knocks on her door woke her up.

"Saira, open the door. What's wrong??" she heard her mom call out, sounding urgent and worried.

Saira quickly gathered her senses and realized she had passed out from the stress of everything that had happened. Just like her phone snaps shut when it runs out of battery, her mind had also snapped shut. This had never happened to her before. Saira quickly called out to her mother and then rushed to the bathroom to wash her face.

"Everyone is waiting for you downstairs. Why aren't you dressed? Did you … just wake up?" her mother sounded half alarmed and half confused, as Saira opened the door of her room.

"Yes, mom. I didn't sleep well last night because Ananya and Pritika and I were facetiming…" Saira blurted out, *"I'll quickly dress up and come downstairs"*, she added to avoid any more questions.

Saira could hear her Bua and Nani downstairs. She slipped into her blue dress–the one she had planned to pose with her 5K balloon and unlike her usual self, she put in minimum effort to dress up. She just wanted to look normal enough to not astound her family with her appearance.

When she hurried down the stairs, she noticed the lobby was dark and quiet. Suddenly, a party popper burst from down below and her family shouted, *"Happy birthday Saira,"* and flicked the lights on.

Something was amiss. It took Saira a whole minute to realise her grandparents and aunts and uncles–EVERYONE–was dressed in blue, while her mom wore a dress just like hers.

"We wanted to give you a real #MeParty," her grandma spoke as she engulfed

her in a big hug. Her grandmother whispered some prayers and kissed her on her forehead, *"I am so thankful to God to have been blessed with a grandchild like you."* As Saira went around and met her family, they all told her how much they loved her and were proud of the person she was becoming.

Her aunts started talking of the time she had first started talking. The conversation quickly moved to her first dance video and Saira felt her entire life being played out through the memories of her family. As these memories flooded the room, they flushed out the toxins of Nat's videos and posts from Saira's mind. Safe in the love of her family, Saira realized how silly she had been to chase Nat all along. She hungrily consumed the love around her and let the hate of the evening drown out of her life, drop by drop.

As the evening wore on, Saira was glad she had left her phone upstairs. She didn't want to think about the video.

"I have recorded it all—for your Insta update," Dad winked at her.

That's it! Saira thought and rushed upstairs, ignoring all notifications. She quickly created a post—not just a story—but something that would stay on her feed forever, unlike all the other stories which would disappear by morning.

She posted the video of her family showering her with love and speaking of her as a baby and wrote, "My #MeParty is thriving, with my fam who genuinely adores and cherishes me, no conditions attached. As for anyone trying to belittle me–cute that you're thinking about me so much, considering I have zero clue who you are. 😂 #PositiveVibes #NotToday

10:30 PM, @SoSaira
*"And a massive shoutout to Nat for reminding me I deserve **so much better***!*"* 

10:35 PM, @SoSaira
As she slipped out of her dress, she looked at herself in the mirror. "Happy 16th birthday, Saira," she whispered to herself. She noticed her best friends–Ananya, Pritika and GG–replied to her story.

@PrettyKa: You know it, bestie! Always got your back. Never forget your worth! ✨ "

@GGame: "Duh! Told ya! So proud of you for owning it. ❤️ "

@Ananyaya: "Exactly what I said! Keep shining, you deserve nothing less. "

She smiled and turned on the alarm clock on her phone. School would begin at 8 AM, and she wouldn't miss it.

My DNA Speaks A Language Only Ma Learned

Ankita Gupta

"What if I were not your daughter but your son, Mom?"

Ma chooses to stay mute, because she knows,

maybe it would've been for the best.

Every day is an option- to speak or not to speak.

Wait no- whether to receive a slap or be a silent witness

and watch your dreams being neatly folded

and presented to your younger brother.

I am merely a temporary guest in my own house,

being fed to be married,

just like Ma was once ritually wed

to this 12"X14" ft. kitchen.

They say, one inherits genes from both parents,

but my DNA speaks a language only Ma learned,

and so did my grandmother,

and my aunt,

and all the ladies in this family.

I inherited not those eyes with colour of after rain soil

or the thick lustrous hair she hides in a braid each morning–

bonded with left lover love on that scrunchie

I gifted her when I was 10.

Instead, I took over, her way of being quiet–just quiet.

Always seen by the gas stove, never heard,

cooking food for family of seven.

The kitchen tap sings the song of water while washing away waste food,

the steel-ware clinks in protest when carried together,

the pressure-cooker quite frequently whistles in tease–

Ma's best friends, all having an individual voice,

encouraging her to speak

but her ears only bend toward the squeak of the kitchen door

every time she enters- announcing her trespass

into her own life.

She has mastered the course on invisibility,

when not to flinch,

when not to blink,

when not to exist.

And as for me?

I've been watching,

learning–to play dumb–an heirloom anklet,

handed down

you can't hear it, unless you're

a woman of this family.

FINDING HOME

Lind Grant-Oyeye

I wish we could talk about birds

and how they migrate in and out

of seasons. The pole they perch on

still standing while oceans give in.

and the woman by the street corner trembles

from all she calls remembrance–

The embracing of what is buried

 what is rising,

 tracing

with greying fingertips,

the tip of trailing dream

 buried in this old mirror–

greying.

Delvis Cortez, *The Cub*

WHERE HOME AND FLOWERS RESIDE

Mariano Moreno

Where is home? Home is a place where one can rest peacefully at night without a worry in the world. In a time where home has come to mean the place where family lies and the ties where one's culturally rich land begin, home is no word described by "defining" in a dictionary. For someone like me, home is where my memories reside and recreate moments with vague sounds of laughter in the walls. Some would say my home is where my loved ones would sing at my birthday parties, others might mean home is where my heritage domains the history of earths and rivers, but I would say my true home is the place I bring with me wherever I go.

I remember being 13 when I began my journal. Our humble ranch was no place for rest and relaxation. Waking up when sunlight split the horizon, walking through the fields and rows of natural fireworks with bright bursts of colorful petals, and listening to the sounds of wild fauna as if my personal orchestra, are all so true and happy memories that my mind might forget by my heart cherishes. Some souls find joy in the percussion like music of running cars and rhythmic footsteps; however, my mind found tranquility in the first few years of my life on that small ranch where the only barrier was that of my own emotions tying me down.

My hands bruised and aching from the constant work, or in actuality my hands kissed and massaged by the tenderness of cotton I constantly picked. Our ranch was without a doubt a pride I carried on my shoulders and a fire that fueled the inner corners of my soul. While watching the clouds fly overhead like the many birds that visited and left, I realized it wasn't just work but a place of wonder. How else would cotton grow as if enchanted by music? How else would cows "moo" and pigs "oink" as if trying to communicate with me. Home was where flowers grew for sure.

At 16 years old, my home had to change. Life began to evolve and interests as well along with this new a metamorphosis. I remember love and its synonyms becoming larger and larger in my vocabulary. This unique word occupied the light in my eyes and enchanted the place around me. Love was my ranch, my ever-sprouting flora, my smile on a rainy day. I met a man who saw me for more than anyone ever had. When storms drowned the beauties I viewed, he would part the clouds to bring warmth back into my life. When no one ever saw me as a child who just wanted to play instead of work, he bought me a doll to tell that little girl who lived inside of me that it's okay to not want to grow up. Home was my ranch but he made me feel home could be anywhere he and I could find happiness together.

It might have been impulsive, but the past is in the past. I packed my bags, kissed my brothers goodbye and had one last longing look at the flowers. By morning I was on my way to a new adventure, a new chapter hopefully full of recurring words such as joy, husband, and children. Although no wedding ring on my finger, hope became a hand I would hold tightly and it would caress my calloused fingers whenever I couldn't tell what the next sentence would tell of my story.

Now 20 years old I found myself writing in this journal again. Far from my ranch, we landed in a small town with nothing but new neighbors and a small house that became what I would now call home. This title wasn't just mine to call because I joyfully shared it with my husband and our new born child. Life is an amazing gift we couldn't wait to share with a new member to our family. Love became the sun and family became the pillars of a new foundation. Great things happened every day and happiness kept me company as my new best friend after hope had fulfilled its duties. From one miracle to the next we welcomed not just one but four babies into our house. While I'll admit it was quite the work to raise a family, how could anything be wrong when my husband was there to assure me life has nothing but gifts and smiles to brighten up our days ahead.

When unsure what to write for a title, always go for the recurring words. That's how I know this piece will be called "nothing but love, family, and joy". What was once rustling leaves now turned into sizzling stoves and nighttime lullabies. My hands were at constant work while my husband went out and supported us financially. Even through chaos this family found peace.

At 22, I grieve in silence. Now me and my four boys, no husband to lift my sorrows. Unfortunate shouldn't be a word my family gets called. Where is my husband to part the clouds and make me smile? Hope is my best friend because I have to look ahead for these four beautiful gifts he left me. Sadness cannot occupy the light in my eyes because this family needs a rock to hold them down.

I called my mother and she came from my ranch to help me with chores and taking care of kids. I will be the one to pull this carriage forward because love will give me a power I knew I had all along.

At 25, I started a garden. I've been missing home for a while and flowers remind me of my ranch where I used to live. My oldest is growing up too fast and his younger brothers seem to always want to catch up. I work 2 jobs with a small lunch break in between. My mother worries but I have to do what I have to do for my children.

At 33, I had an accident. I was too sleepy and a machine caught my hand and broke a few fingers. I went to the doctor and they did the best they could but maybe it wasn't enough. Although the world is working against me, I need to continue because I love this family too much to not keep looking towards the horizon for them.

I'm 70, and my children have all grown up. I couldn't be prouder of their lives. They've grown and called new places home. I left my old house and now live with one of my sons. I planted a garden in his front yard to remind me of the importance of finding the important things in life that keep you going. I know my husband isn't here anymore to tell our children he's proud of them, but I'll repeat it to them and my grandkids for as long as I can until they don't need me to remind them anymore. Hopefully that day will never come.

- 64 -

I'm somewhere. I don't remember my age and I can't understand the words around me. Phrases and languages have become blurry and my sense of direction is upside down. I don't see my flowers anymore but I know deep down it was their time to finally rest peacefully. I see a bright firework in the sky made of colorful petals in oranges and yellows. Love fuels the tears in people's eyes and hope carries them forward.

I'm 25, and I started a garden. I was getting home sick so I took a piece of home with me. I hope my children visit their "used to be" home once in a while, and I pray they look at the flowers and remember how proud of them I am. I'm 70 years old and I planted a garden because my true home is the place I bring with me wherever I go.

A MEMORY OF MORTON ST.

Sammy Jo Cienfuegos

when thinking of home, i think of my mother cutting up nopales
and my dad sitting in his leather recliner with his feet up.
i think of how the nopales came from a small cutting from
my paternal grandmother's backyard,
which is now growing in my backyard,
and i really enjoy how she can still exist alongside us in this way,
which is weird,
because i was not particularly close to my paternal grandmother.
but i still think of her when i think of home.

it is so comforting to think about how something so grand
i.e. the row of cacti growing in the backyard
came from something so small and will only continue to grow, much like me.
continuing to grow and grow,
until our roots infiltrate the concrete and cause a pipe to burst.

i'm not sure why i am not as close to my dad's side of the family.
i remember christmases there and pan dulce always being in the kitchen.
every kitchen.
i remember chihuahuas and the smell of cheap beer.
but my cousin's baby is now pregnant and

my quietest uncle has passed away.
and i'm not sure when that happened. but it did. and it continues to.
i'm not sure when time became so cruel. but it's been more painful as of late.
i feel it nick me as it shoves me out of its way.
its covered in espinas and the ink from discarded security tags,
reminding me of its constant presence,
marking me forever.

when i think about my paternal grandmother, i think of the many missed
opportunities for connection. i think of how we were never really able to see
eye to eye,
speaking two different tongues, communicating through smoke signals.
when i think of my mom, and my dad,
i think of how our roles of "parent" and "child" have often been reassigned,
and how i found myself meeting my father when he was four years old
and my mom when she was fourteen.
i have met them at different stages of their life, just as they have met me in
mine.

although cruel, time can sometimes be forgiving in that way,
healing wounds long forgotten, perhaps even healing wounds that are yet to
come.
it's a never ending coil and i have bent the metal at the points i want to
remember
at the cost of distorting what is yet to come.

EL MAÍZ, LA MESTIZA, Y YO

Ahitza Roque

El Maíz, La Mestiza y Yo

El Maíz, La Mestiza y Yo

"Like an ear of corn—a female seed-bearing organ—the mestiza is tenacious, tightly wrapped in the husks of her culture. Like kernels she clings to the cob; with thick stalks and strong brace roots, she holds tight to the earth—she will survive the crossroads"
Borderlands/La Frontera - *Gloria Anzaldúa*

I stand here tall

Raised from the ground
of the Rio Grande Valley

The same soil that raised
generations of
My family

The seed I once was
Worked and Tended

Molded by
Our Rich Traditions,
Love,
and Strength

When you grow up in a field
of genetic reflections
the beauty
of your history
is never lost on you

My food is our food
My accent is our accent
Our field
Our language
Our soil
My home

The seed I once was
is now taller than ever
With the strongest husk
and a stronger mind

And in the blink of an eye
I am off
Intended to be fertilized by
A new soil
Of diverse backgrounds
And endless opportunities

But I arrive and
There's a lot less maize than
I thought

And my accent is "weird"
and
My language is unwelcome

My traditions
My story
My flavor

Different
Exotic
Consumable

They pick me off my stem
And judge
The lusciousness
Of my kernels

The strength of
My roots
Threaten their idea of
what and where
Corn should be

It's Maize

but They say corn.

They care more about
what I am
Than who

And take more of me
Than I know how to give

I stay up at night
And wonder if
I am worth
The work
it took me to get here

Work

Real Blood
Sweat
And Tears

Work

Protesting and boycotting
Organizing and educating
Fighting and winning

Work

Done by the mazes of maize
Found in the genetic library
Of my mind, body,
and soul

Work

Whose history has
sustained me

Ripened me

Before I knew to
thank Them

I thank Them

For protecting my home
and protecting my family
From the Famine of Freedoms
Most of them
couldn't escape

Fighting for
My right to
stand as tall as I do

As loud as I do

And as the sun rises
I send a prayer
And seek the strength
I know is in me
because
It was in Them

I was designed
for preservation
and can provide
sustenance
for generations

My work is not done
Our history is not behind us

They will try and try
To bury me alive
But I will go
Kicking and screaming
As they shove dirt
In my face

Because I was once a seed
And I can and will
Grow again

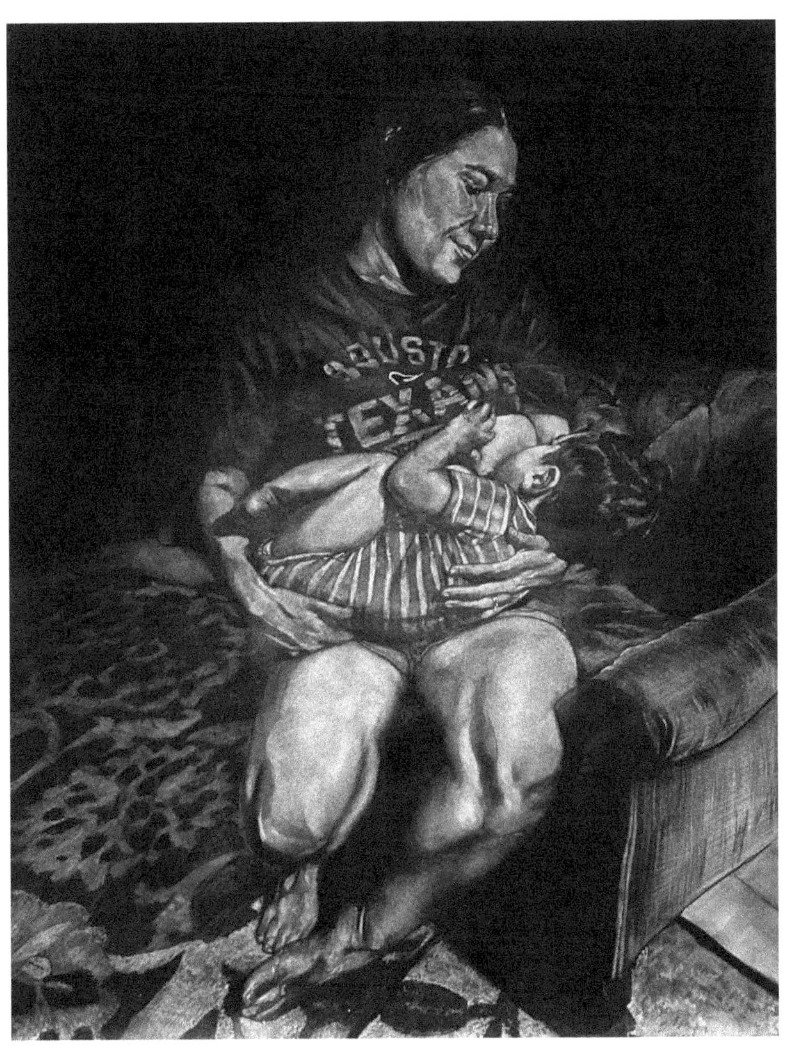

Delvis Cortez, *Mother And Child*

Delvis Cortez, *Gonzalez*

INHOLITOPAISKI

Jessi Farfan

choctaws came from the belly of the earth
we were not born, not made
we emerged from the mother mound
with swamp water pouring from our mouths
and sunlight burning our eyes clean

we climbed out of our mother
towards the cave entrance with our hands bleeding
lungs full of peat
crawling toward our first breath

after we were forced from her breast
without allowing us to wean
they fenced her off
and called her prehistoric
put a plaque off 393
and said she used to matter to us

they built a playground on top of her
made it so you can have your wedding there
or maybe your kid's 6th birthday party
they commodified what's sacred
so white mouths could stomach our story
and give it three stars on travel sites

nanih waiya remakes us
again and again
she spits us out one by one like seeds

the mound is not a mother
not really
she does not cradle
she ruptures
she shoves us from her hearth and
she says *chi pisa la chike*

if you come close enough to listen
put your ear to the dirt
you won't hear a heartbeat
you'll hear us turning over
getting ready
to rise again

BLURS

Jonathan Ramirez

I swallowed American culture
before I learned how to chew it.
Teeth nibbling at my fingertips,
tasting everything I touched:
a wooden desk, yellow pencil,
a slice of navy blue, of self,
and so on. Flavors
propelling me deeper into
the no-return where every
new door locked the one before.
The story blurs between crossings
and prayers, tongues devouring letters
and country-lines.

Two months after my birth,
our story blurs indefinitely.
The family returns to where
belonging comes as a birthright
before freedom is reduced to one
bedroom apartments across a
border asking where do I find the
key that leads back to my origin?
By now I'm school-aged and know
words are a knife hanging from my
teeth, ready to rupture through
prayers from moons ago. So I
remain silent and the river goes.

The river is brave. It speaks some
hybrid language, past and present.
Which do you understand? Its waves,
tainted with dissimilation, language
misconfiguration, and paperwork
push ashore a scene of a family starting new.
Will this land nurture me the way the water
nurtured my parents, the way dirt nurtured
those who came before me? Doctor, my
knees and palms bear the marks of a youth
on gravel, but my voice is a tool yet to
reach the sun. I want to tell the story
again.

When asked why did
your family's route to the
USA proceed as it did?
An ocean pulls me in.
I was young, reeling
through cracked sidewalks,
falling stars crumbling beneath
my feet, a motorcycle that left
its claws on my nose, unforgiving
floods and droughts, dreams all
resurfaced and claimed to be
the beginning. But where to start
with this story?

It's 2006 across the Rio Bravo.
My grandmother sits us outside
Tia Silvia's porch under God's
evening to recount her stories.
The night fabric populates with
stars as she weaves her words
into tales, her voice soft and
maternal. Even years later we
found — the adults smoking, my
cousins and I listening, the palm
trees swaying around us, witnessing —
a way of keeping our history alive.
Slowly, this story will blur.

One last time, our story blurs
in knee-deep waters, chronicles of
an education in a language foreign
to our mouth, a shining set of teeth.
Tongues unfolding, uncomfortable,
unlearning, and then learning, again
to pronounce our names. New sounds
losing me, piecing me together. But
who you are will always remain.
In the evening, I whisper prayers into
the waters, and by dawn, they find their
way back to me: You will make this river
your bed. You will tell this story again.

A Library on Mango Street:
"Reach and Do Not Forget to Reach"

R. Joseph Rodríguez

"Art is in all of us."

These six words kept me company after I found them as part of Sandra Cisneros's biographical note in the first edition of *The House on Mango Street*. The novel was published in 1984 in my home city, Houston, Texas, by Arte Público Press at the University of Houston. However, it would not be until 1990, as an adolescent, that I found the novel in the Houston Public Library for my reading.

Like Cisneros, my siblings and I are benefactors of public libraries and the vast amount of storytelling and resources offered to patrons across the country. I still remember finding the shelved, worn copy with cover art by Alejandro Romero. I was drawn to the book cover that resembled some of the streets of Magnolia Park, or the East End, where we lived. Art thus became a possibility to tell stories in my head and on paper and to document the lives surrounding my very own.

When I was younger, my family's Saturday mornings were spent at the neighborhood library. I remember those mornings as a shared ritual. When my father was not working at the oil refinery in nearby Pasadena, we would ride the Ford pick-up truck to the Nena E. Stanaker Branch Library. Other times, my mother, my two oldest sisters, my older brother and I held hands tightly on our walk to the library. We clutched our books with our free hands and kept our library cards deep in our pockets. I looked forward to the hand-in-hand stroll to the house of books, the library, which held so much intellect, creativity, and imagination.

Years later, I would learn that Cisneros also experienced public libraries in Chicago that were welcoming her and her family—across diverse interests and world cultures and languages.

To Be and Be

To this day, I remember my favorite reading spot in the old Stanaker Branch Library. In this area there were no large chairs or tables, but furnishings for those of us who had tiny bodies and a big imagination. The library smelled sweet, as if the books were leather-bound. Like the incense of Immaculate Heart of Mary Church, the library offered its own scent as a place for learning: a safe, brave space.

Even as I grew older into young adulthood, I found a space to explore, imagine, and be. One of the book signings I have by Cisneros declares in large cursive: "Para el Joseph Rodríguez: Be and be and be and be!"

Moreover, in the Houston Public Library is where I found a novel that guided me to imagine many more worlds in this one and that was *The House on Mango Street.* My very own neighborhood and its people came alive on the printed page. Never had my own life—or the neighborhood I inhabited with my family—appeared as inspiration and possibility for the creative and literary arts.

Indeed, it was reassuring to read Cisneros's essay "Ghosts and Voices: Writing from Obsession" in which she reveals her love for the book *The Little House* by Virginia Lee Burton. The book changed her life and offered more ways of seeing the world, much like *The House of Mango Street* did for me. Cisneros writes, "I read and reread that book, sometimes taking the book out of the library seven times in a row. Once my brother and I even schemed to keep it" (71). These two experiences came together in my own formation as a reader and years later to become a teacher and writer for adolescents to guide them to the worlds created by Cisneros. In the essay "Living as a Writer: Choice and Circumstance," Cisneros reveals what she calls a "life in literature" and acknowledges the privileges her parents made available and states:

> Because of my mother, I had a library card before I learned to read and thereafter our bookless house was filled with books, albeit borrowed. Because of my mother[,] I spent my childhood afternoons in my room reading instead of the kitchen. My mother allowed me this luxury for some inexplicable reason even though I was/am an only daughter in a family of six sons. (8).

Cisneros's candid voice found in her essays can nurture an emerging writer to persist in letters, despite the challenges, hardships, and cultural traditions one confronts to become and belong, and that was the case for me as a young reader and library patron.

Along with the lessons I learned as a student in the local Houston ISD schools, my library time fostered the learning of two languages side by side: English and Spanish. Neither one was better.

Instead, the two languages coexisted. I remember learning to read and write and coming to value the linguistic and cultural richness of both languages through the books written by Cisneros and interviews and recordings with her that confirmed the need for honoring our communities, languages, and stories.

For instance, English flowed in the library, side by side with Spanish. *Leche.* Milk. *Lluvia.* Rain. *Piña.* Pineapple. *Perro.* Dog. Little did I know that English, Spanish, the public library, and *The House on Mango Street* would transform my thinking, my writing—my life. Our library's programming was also rich with storytellers and musicians. Young people's literature and book characters came to life before our eyes as a young woman strummed the strings of an old guitar and sang with deep, guttural sounds in English and Spanish. A storyteller taught us how to turn the pages of a book. Before turning the page, she ran her hand across the page as if she were reading it in Braille.

She explained: "Turn the pages like this. From the corner. Not with dog paws or cat licks, but with care."

We learned that books have backs, spines. Just like us.

"A book with a bad back is ruined forever," she said. (I wanted to tell her that my Papi still worked, even though his back ached every day from manual labor, but she was already ahead of me, turning the page, gliding a finger across the picture book's spine.)

In an essay "The Patterson Public Library" about her girlhood in New Jersey, Judith Ortiz Cofer reveals, "A library is my sanctuary, and I am always at home in one" (134). And so, it was for me and many readers who recognized the literary merit and contributions by Cisneros to US and world letters upon finding her work (Author).

During the late 1980s and 1990s, our library's bookshelves began to reflect the diverse readership in the East End and the greater United States. Spanish and indigenous surnames appeared on the spines of books and on the covers of periodicals. Texts by US Latinx authors were shelved alongside the Eurocentric classics as contemporary classics. A democratic library was emerging before my eyes as I read about the world in which I lived and yearned to contribute as an emerging poet and writer.

For example, I read a picture book *A Birthday Basket for Tía* (1993) by Pat Mora and Cecily Lang about a young girl named Cecilia who prepares for her beloved great-aunt named Ignacia's ninetieth birthday. This was the first children's book I'd read about extended families like mine and then followed by Cisneros's *Hairs: Pelitos* (1994) with art illustrations by Terry Ybáñez. The more I read, the more I realized that my universe found a place in print with readers ready to be affirmed and guided. The world of books no longer seemed so distant or irrelevant to my existence, but relatable with characters named Alicia, Edna, Elenita, Geraldo, and Meme, among others.

The People's University

Even today as I return to my neighborhood library, which is a newly designed building, I recognize how this special house of books fostered a lasting relationship between book and reader and introduced me to Cisneros's novels, poetry, stories, and essays. Ralph Waldo Emerson called the library the "People's University." Historically, public libraries in this country have been the people's most accessible university. Most importantly, public libraries serve the organic intellectual: a diverse citizenry of readers and thinkers of all ages, backgrounds, colors, and interests.

Years ago, I entered the library as a young reader, like Cisneros, eager to introduce meaning into my world, and the world I would later enter as a university student and educator. Walking through the doors of the Stanaker Branch Library all those years ago, as a child and then an adolescent, has led me to many successes and challenges. Most importantly, the library introduced me to Mango Street and a body of literature that transformed my way of being, thinking, and understanding.

In *Sandra Cisneros in the Classroom* (2002), Carol Jago explains, "Like Pip [Philip Pirrip], Esperanza [Cordero] refuses to be defined by the circumstances that surround her. Like Charles Dickens, Sandra Cisneros offers readers a fictional world so rich in detail that we know what it feels like to walk down Paulina [Street] and to sit on those tight little steps" (xii). Art created possibilities and futures that began with Cisneros's words and characters as well as the power to notice the stories within my own family—some known, while others still unspoken.

One vignette that stood out was "Four Skinny Trees" and the message that Esperanza believes the trees reveal—if we are to pause and notice—offered guidance and comfort as I came of age:

> When I am too sad and too skinny to keep keeping, when I am a tiny thing against so many bricks, then it is I look at trees. When there is nothing left to look at on this street. Four who grew despite concrete. Four who reach and do not forget to reach. Four whose only reason is to be and be. (75)

The public library is a safe and brave haven for learning and exploring. I reached to connect and found many more worlds through a library on Mango Street and beyond. The books I find there shape my intellect and imagination. For me, the public library fosters a kind of book communion—one that is necessary for the cultivation of my interior life and for the arts and humanities.

 **Sandra Cisneros**

Dear R. Joseph Rodríguez,
We were all very thrilled to
get your letter of high praise —
my editor, agent, and my translator.
Thank you for taking the time to
write such an exquisite letter of
encouragement — esp. in light that
the book is just out. A wonderful

Author's correspondence with Sandra Cisneros about her Spanish-

language version of the short fiction collection *Woman Hollering Creek*

and Other Stories, which affirms Mexican-origin cultural heritages and

identities.

Works Cited

Cisneros, Sandra. *El arroyo de la Llorona y otros cuentos*. Translated by

Liliana Valenzuela, Vintage Español, 1996.

—. "From a Writer's Notebook, Ghosts and Voices: Writing from

Obsession." *The Américas Review*, vol. 15, no. 1, Spring 1987, pp. 69-

73.

—. *The House on Mango Street*. Arte Público P, 1984.

—. *The House on Mango Street*. Vintage Contemporaries 1984.

—. "Living as a Writer: Choice and Circumstance." *Feminist Writers

Guild*, vol. 10, no. 1, Feb. 1987, pp. 8-9.

—. *Woman Hollering Creek and Other Stories*. Random House, 1991.

Cisneros, Sandra, and Terry Ybáñez. *Hairs: Pelitos*. Penguin Random

House, 1994.

Jago, Carol. *Sandra Cisneros in the Classroom: "Do Not Forget to Reach."*

National Council of Teachers of English, 2002.

Mora, Pat, and Cecily Lang. *A Birthday Basket for Tía*. Macmillan, 1993.

Ortiz Cofer, Judith. *The Latin Deli: Prose and Poetry*. U of Georgia P,

1993.

Rodríguez, R. Joseph. *Youth Scribes: Teaching a Love of Writing*.

Heinemann, 2025.

Contributors

Daylen K. Adams: Daylen K. Adams is decorated combat veteran, who dedicated years to our country earning the rank of Sergeant First Class in the Army. After retiring from the military, with multiple injuries and PTSD he faced significant challenges reintegrating into the workforce. Daylen continues to break barriers and be a community leader in the RGV.

Sammy Jo Cienfuegos: Sammy Jo Cienfuegos has her roots planted in Brownsville, TX. She was named the "Outstanding Graduate in Writing and Rhetoric" at St. Edward's University. She is a journalist, editor, and grant consultant. In her spare time, she enjoys reading, practicing yoga, and going on adventures with her dog, Ollie.

Delvis Cortez: Cortez is an Edcouch, Texas native who's interest in Visual Art began at an early age. Of course, every child doodles, draws and colors but his was an internal drive that later proved to be a way of being and having earned a bachelor's degree in Visual Art with an emphasis in Painting. Currently, Cortez is focused on figurative works done in charcoal or graphite that explore scale, composition, and mood, with a perspective shaped by his upbringing in South Texas and an interest in The Old Masters. He credits his loving wife and son, Veronica and Luke for their valuable support and love.

Jessi Farfan: Jessi Farfan is a Choctaw writer who thinks blood quantum should be illegal and sarcasm should count as medicine. She loves to write poems that make your fingers sweat and smudge those fake colonial borders. Their work can be found in MORIA, Lucky Jefferson, and Mouthful of Salt.

Lind Grant-Oyeye: Lind Grant-Oyeye is a Nigerian-born poet whose work explores identity, heritage, and the nuances of human experience. Her voice blends cultural insight with lyrical depth, resonating across continents. With multiple published collections, Lind continues to carve a space for thoughtful, evocative poetry in today's global literary landscape.

Ankita Gupta: Adv. Ankita Gupta is a practicing lawyer with experience before the Supreme Court of India and several High Courts of India, currently pursuing her Masters In Law. Her interest in writing predates her legal career and continues to develop both within and beyond the courtroom. She recently gave wings to her dreams by publishing her debut poetry book- Love's Grammar which is available on all digital book-selling platforms. A few of her poems have also been published in regional literary magazines, including *SpillWords Press* and *Delhi Poetry Slam*.

Neha Gupta: Neha Gupta is a literacy facilitator by the day, stationed at the school library, tasked with reading and thinking aloud with 6–10 years old children. Her afternoons are spent juggling chores and parenting her two children. She tries to squeeze in a nap, while also trying to read through a book and then review it on the gram. Sometimes, though, she gives in to temptation and only escapes the burdening pile of life's endless demands with Netflix. In the late evening, when her children are sufficiently tired, she packs them off to sleep–and finally sits down to write. Later, snoring lightly, she dreams of another life - a life, in which she is a published author and reads and thinks aloud parts of her own books to an audience of a different kind.

Kendra Lara: Kendra Lara is a recent 2025 MFA graduate from UTRGV. Born and raised in Texas, her work incorporates many aspects of Mexican American culture. This piece, "I am a No Sabo kid" shows the internal struggle of wanting to connect and understand the other part of oneself.

Alexis M. Levine: Alexis M. Levine is a Kenyan poet and novelist who writes on topics often left in the dark. In her free time, she's usually buried in books, playing the piano, or listening to music, drawing inspiration for her writing from the world around her.

Luis Lizardo: Luis Lizardo is an RGV-based writer and musician. Their work spans fiction, poetry, and song, blending lyrical language with emotional depth. They explore fantastical concepts through the lens of the mundane, humanizing wonder through lived experience. Why I Wait by the River marks their debut literary publication with more on the horizon. Follow along on Instagram @lizardocreates.

Robinson Lopez: Robinson Lopez is an Austin-based photographer and archivist with roots from Dallas to Laredo. His ancestry intersects Spanish colonization, White Southern settlement, Mexican revolution, and mid-century politics. Weaving together Anglo and Tejano identity, uncovers how conquest, faith, and adversity answer the question, "How Texan am I?"

Martin E. Marizcal: An RGV native, Martin E. Marizcal graduated from Texas State University—San Marcos in 2015. In the interim, he has mainly worked in construction around the country. He enjoys a benign addiction to coffee, casual yardwork, music and movies and books and games, cats, and cooking for friends and family.

Mariano Moreno: Mariano Moreno is a young author of the Rio Grande Valley and high school student at Valley View. Mariano finds his passion for writing in his culture and community as he plans to continue to use his biliterate and bilingual abilities to write impactful stories that need to be told.

Richard Quiroz: Richard Quiroz is a Librarian, reader, and writer from South Texas. He graduated from TAMU-CC with a BA in English in May of 2021 and from UNT with a master's in library science in December of 2023. He enjoys learning about history, watching horror movies, and visiting museums and local historical sites.

Jonathan Ramirez: Jonathan Ramirez is a writer and educator based in the Rio Grande Valley. His chapbook, Snow Year, was published in 2024 with Ethel Zine Press. In his free time, Ramirez can be found going on walks with his earphones on blasting pop music.

R. Joseph Rodríguez: R. Joseph Rodríguez is the author of Youth Scribes: Teaching a Love of Writing. He teaches reading language arts at an early college high school. Joseph and his students read banned, challenged, censored, and confiscated books—from the classics to contemporary classics. He lives and teaches in Austin and Fredericksburg, Texas.

Ahitza Roque: Born and raised in the Rio Grande Valley, Ahitza Roque is a poet and 5th grade teacher. She turns to poetry to understand and reflect on the world around her. In the classroom, she hopes to nurture that same love for words and expression in her students.

www.ingramcontent.com/pod-product-compliance
Lightning Source LLC
Chambersburg PA
CBHW040837010826
48978CB00012BB/798